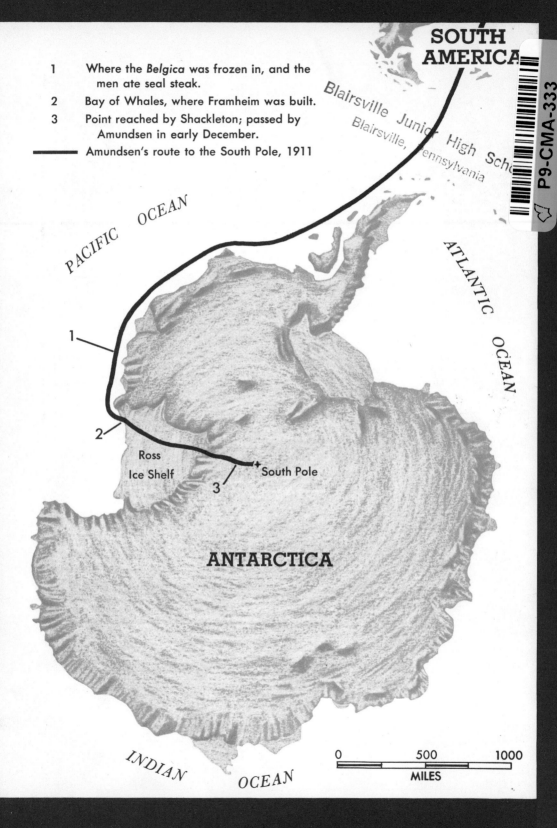

1   Where the *Belgica* was frozen in, and the men ate seal steak.
2   Bay of Whales, where Framheim was built.
3   Point reached by Shackleton; passed by Amundsen in early December.
——   Amundsen's route to the South Pole, 1911

SOUTH AMERICA

PACIFIC OCEAN

ATLANTIC OCEAN

Ross Ice Shelf

South Pole

ANTARCTICA

INDIAN OCEAN

0   500   1000
MILES

 THE ASTROLABE, an instrument developed by the Greeks, is the symbol for World Explorer Books. At the time of Columbus, sailors used the astrolabe to chart a ship's course. The arm across the circle could be moved to line up with the sun or a star. Using the number indicated by the pointer, a sailor could tell his approximate location on the sea. Although the astrolabe was not completely accurate, it helped many early explorers in their efforts to conquer the unknown.

World Explorer Books are written especially for children who love adventure and exploration into the unknown. Designed for young readers, each book has been tested by the Dale-Chall readability formula. Leo Fay, Ph.D., Professor of Education at Indiana University, is educational consultant for the series. Dr. Fay, an experienced teacher and lecturer, is well known for his professional bulletins and text material in both elementary reading and social studies.

A WORLD EXPLORER

Roald Amundsen

BY CATEAU DeLEEUW

ILLUSTRATED BY GEORGE I. PARRISH

GARRARD PUBLISHING COMPANY
CHAMPAIGN, ILLINOIS

To
Anne Johansen,
Tippy's Norwegian friend.
(And mine, too, I hope!)

This series is edited by Elizabeth Minot Graves

Contents

1

A Determined Boy

Roald Amundsen sat reading a book in his home in Oslo, Norway. It was the winter of 1887. His breath came fast with excitement.

"What are you reading?" asked his mother as she stood behind him.

"A book about Sir John Franklin, the Arctic explorer," Roald answered.

"You should be studying your lessons," his mother said. "You are twelve years old. If you are to become a doctor, you must learn a great deal."

"But I don't want to become a doctor!" Roald cried.

His mother frowned. "You are going to be a doctor, whether you want it or not," she said firmly. "I have decided it."

Roald knew she would have her way. He would spend his whole life doing something he did not want to do. Roald had only one wish. He wanted to be an explorer like Sir John Franklin.

He made one more try. "I want to be an explorer," he said, "not a doctor. I want to find the North Pole."

His mother laughed. "Don't be silly! That takes a great deal of money and experience. It takes courage and bold planning, too." She took his book from him and looked at it. "Sir John Franklin's

life. Hmp! And what happened to him?
He starved to death in the Arctic."

Roald reached for the book, but she
held it away from him. He hunted for
words to answer her. They were hard to
find.

Though his family had a shipping
business, they were not rich. Perhaps
some day he could raise the money he
would need. Of course he had no
experience in exploring. But that would
come in time. He knew, too, that he had
courage. And he would learn to plan.

Roald's father was dead. His older
brothers had left home to make their
way in the world. Only Roald was left
with his mother. She was a determined
woman, but Roald was determined too.
From then on, he kept his ambition a
secret.

He felt he should begin training for
his future. Because an Artic explorer had
to have strong muscles, Roald played
soccer. He did not like soccer, but the
game toughened him.

He practiced his skiing, always making
the most difficult runs. To harden his
body he slept with his bedroom windows
wide open. The winters were terribly cold
in Norway. His mother scolded him.

"You will make yourself sick," she said. She closed his windows with a bang. "Why do you do such foolish things?"

Roald waited until she had left his room. Then he opened the windows again. If he wanted to find the North Pole, he would have to be able to stand the cold.

Everything he did fitted into his plan for the future. Roald had made up his mind to become an Arctic explorer.

2

Lost in the Snow

When Roald Amundsen was twenty, his mother died. At once he left the University where he had been studying to be a doctor.

One day Amundsen said to a friend, "Let's cross the plain west of Oslo."

His friend looked at him. "Now? In midwinter? No one has ever done it!"

"Yes, now," Amundsen said. His eyes were shining. "It's only 75 miles or so."

The high plain was used by Lapp herdsmen in the summer for their reindeer, but no one lived on it. In winter it was deserted.

"We can start at Mogen, the farmhouse on this side. If we allow ourselves two days, we can reach Garen, the farmhouse on the western side. I am sure we can do it."

Amundsen's friend agreed to try. They went by ski to Mogen. When the farmers learned Amundsen's plan, they said, "It can't be done."

"We'll do it," Amundsen said.

He wanted to set out the next morning, but a blizzard came up in the night. For eight days Amundsen and his friend waited for the snow to stop falling.

At last they could set out across the plain. Each carried a reindeer sleeping

bag. They had no tent. A few crackers, some butter, and some chocolate bars were their only food. They had a compass and a map.

They knew that there was a herders' hut in the middle of the plain. When they reached it that evening, they were tired and hungry. To their dismay, the door and the window had been nailed up tightly.

They had no tools, but they finally got in. Amundsen climbed to the roof and took the boards off the chimney so they could have a fire. It was very cold, and another storm had come up.

They found a small sack of flour. "We'll make porridge out of this, and save our own food," Amundsen said.

For two days they stayed in the hut, then they skied on. It was still snowing, and the wet snow destroyed their map. They did not find the farm Garen.

When night came, they had to camp out in the open. Yet Amundsen liked being in his wet sleeping bag in the cold. He remembered how the Franklin expedition had suffered.

He did not feel so cheerful the next morning, when they found their sacks of food had vanished. This was serious. They hurried toward the west, hoping to find Garen.

The snow was so thick they could see nothing ahead. "Shall we turn back?" Amundsen asked his friend.

"Y-yes." His companion's teeth were chattering from cold and lack of food.

That night Amundsen made himself a small cave in the snow. This kept the wind out. When he woke in the night he could not move! A huge block of ice had frozen around him.

He could scarcely breathe. "Help! Help!" he called. His friend did not hear him.

When his friend awoke, he could not find Amundsen. It was still night. Finally he saw a small piece of fur. It belonged to Amundsen's sleeping bag. It took three hours for his friend to dig him out.

Now they were both weak. The snow had stopped, so they found their direction by the stars. Suddenly Amundsen's friend disappeared! He had fallen off a cliff, and landed on a ledge. Amundsen pulled him up.

They waited for daylight before they went on. They stopped at every lake and stream to drink water. That helped their hunger a little.

It was getting dark when Amundsen called out, "There is a shed!" He skied quickly toward it. It was filled with hay. There were ski tracks around it.

"Look!" He showed the tracks to his friend. "We must be near a farm. That means people—food—warmth!"

His friend was too tired to go on. They burrowed into the hay and slept.

The next morning they found they were only an hour from Mogen. The farmer and his family did not recognize them when they entered the little house. The young men were thin and hollow-eyed. They looked like scarecrows.

A year later they made a discovery. When they had turned back they had been a few hundred feet from their goal! The farmer at Garen had been puzzling over their ski tracks for months.

When Amundsen and his friend parted, Amundsen said, "It was a great adventure, wasn't it? Just like Arctic exploration."

"If that was Arctic exploration, you can have it," his friend said.

Amundsen smiled. "I'll take it," he said. He was more sure than ever of what he wanted to do.

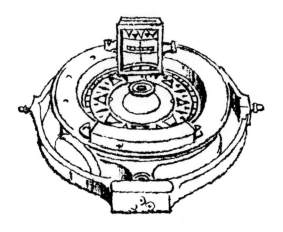

3

His First Expedition

Amundsen decided that he must get a ship captain's license. That would be the next step in preparing himself for polar exploration.

He had read of explorers who had had trouble because their leader was not also the captain of their ship. This would not happen to him!

First he sailed on a ship in the North Atlantic. Then he signed up as first mate for a scientific expedition on the *Belgica*. It was going to the Antarctic to study the Southern Magnetic Pole.

Compasses do not point to the true, or geographic, North and South Poles. Instead they point to the Magnetic Poles. These are over a thousand miles from the true Poles.

Amundsen, two scientists, and Dr. Cook, the ship's doctor, were to be left upon the Antarctic continent for the winter. They would make scientific studies there. The *Belgica* would pick them up again in the spring.

When the ship reached the Antarctic, a great storm arose. The *Belgica* was blown a hundred miles inside a field of ice cakes. Before it could get out, the cakes froze together. Now the ship was held fast for the winter, or longer.

"I am very worried about the crew," Amundsen told his friend, Dr. Cook. "They haven't proper winter clothing, and the food supplies are small. There isn't even enough fuel for the lamps. It will be dark for months on end."

He was right to be worried. The commander of the expedition did not know that men have to have fresh food, even in the frozen Antarctic. Almost everyone became sick with scurvy.

Amundsen and Dr. Cook spent hours hunting seals and penguins. They dragged them to the ship for food. But the commander did not like the taste of the meat. He would not let the men eat it. Finally the commander and the captain became so sick they had to stay in bed.

21

Now Amundsen was in command. The first thing he did was to dig the dead seals out of the snow. He and Dr. Cook cut steaks from them.

"Cook these as fast as you can," they told the cook.

Everyone ate the steaks, even the commander. Within a week, the men were much better.

They still had no warm clothing.

Amundsen found a store of bright red blankets. "Just the thing," he said to Dr. Cook. "I shall have them made into suits for the men."

When the sailors appeared on deck in the red blanket-suits, everyone burst out laughing. It was happy laughter, though. The men were warm for the first time in weeks.

For thirteen months the *Belgica* was

frozen fast. When the Antarctic summer came, they still could not get out.

Dr. Cook had noticed places where the ice seemed thinner. He had the men explode dynamite in these places. A narrow path opened through the ice and at last they were free.

The *Belgica* was the first expedition to have wintered in the Antarctic. Amundsen felt he had learned several important things about living in the polar regions. And he could get his captain's license now. That meant he was one step nearer his goal—the North Pole.

"What's next?" a friend asked him soon after he returned to Norway.

"My own ship and my own crew," Amundsen said. He added slowly, "And my own decisions."

4

Uncharted Waters

"We're off!" Amundsen said softly.

The shores of Norway slipped out of sight. The night closed in on his tiny ship, the *Gjoa*. It had taken almost four years for this moment to come.

In these four years Amundsen had studied magnetic science and astronomy. He had bought and outfitted his ship, and gathered together a crew of six devoted men. The famous explorer Fridtjof

Nansen had helped him. Amundsen was proud of Nansen's help. Nansen had been a hero to him for years.

Amundsen thought back to the hard times behind him. "Why do you want to find the Northwest Passage?" people had asked him. "There's no need of it any more. That was a dream in the days when men were trying to find an easier way to the Orient."

"Perhaps my trip through the Northwest Passage will open up new ideas in science," Amundsen would say.

Men had explored the northern shores of Canada by land. Other men had sailed past some of the islands there. They knew there was a waterway from the Atlantic Ocean to the Pacific Ocean. But no one had ever sailed it.

Amundsen wanted to be the first to

navigate the passage. More important, he planned to study the Northern Magnetic Pole. He would study the Eskimos too.

At Greenland they took on twenty sledge dogs, more gasoline, and more food. The trip would take at least two years, perhaps three. There was no place where they could buy supplies once they had left Greenland.

After Greenland, the *Gjoa* headed west to the islands in the Arctic Sea north of Canada's mainland. They came to Beechey Island. It was here that Amundsen's boyhood hero, Sir John Franklin, had wintered on his last expedition. Franklin had died trying to find the Northwest Passage.

Soon after they left Beechey Island fog covered the sea with a veil. They knew there were islands on either side of them,

but they could not see them. The *Gjoa* crept along slowly. Once she struck a rock, but soon got off it.

That night a shout rang out. "Fire!"

Amundsen leaped up. "Where?"

"In the engine room!"

The men rushed to get pails of sea water. If the fire spread to the gasoline tanks, the ship would be blown up. Luckily the men were in time. They put the fire out.

Two days later they ran aground again. The waves smashed the little ship against the rocks. Amundsen wondered if she would break into pieces. The men threw heavy cases of cargo into the sea to lighten the *Gjoa*. When the high tide came, they managed to float free.

They anchored off the coast to repair the ship. A strong gale began to blow.

Amundsen feared the ship would be blown onto the beach and broken up.

"Keep the engine going," he ordered. "Head into the wind. Then perhaps our anchor will hold."

For four days and nights they kept the engine running. At last the gale blew itself out, and the *Gjoa* went on. She rounded the eastern shore of King William Island. Amundsen looked to the west. That way lay the Northwest Passage. But the Northern Magnetic Pole came first. He believed it was in this area.

Lieutenant Hansen was in the crow's nest, high on the mast. He called, "I see the finest little harbor in the world!"

Amundsen climbed aloft. "You are right," he said firmly. "This is where we will winter. We will call this place Gjoahavn."

5

Eskimo Friends

Winter in the Arctic is long and dark and cold. It was September when the *Gjoa* came to rest in Gjoahavn. Amundsen knew they would have to work fast to build the shelters for their scientific instruments. With these instruments they would study the Northern Magnetic Pole.

There were no trees on this Arctic island, so there was no wood. The

buildings were made from the wooden packing cases in which their instruments and food had been packed.

When the buildings were finished, Amundsen said, "Now we must have kennels for the dogs." The dogs started to bark and howl as if they understood him. "See?" he laughed. "They know that winter is almost here. They don't want to stay out in the cold."

Last of all they built a hut for the two
scientists who would study the Magnetic
Pole. The rest of the men would live on
the *Gjoa*.

"Next," Amundsen said with a pleased
smile, "we must have fresh meat—enough
to last us the winter."

The best hunters went off to shoot
caribou—the American reindeer. Before
long there was a great pile of meat.

They did not need refrigerators. The weather froze the meat for them!

One day they thought they saw more caribou in the distance. Hansen took a a second look. "If these are caribou," he said, "they are walking on two legs instead of four!"

"Eskimos!" Amundsen cried. "I had hoped we would have Eskimo visitors."

He had promised the scientists in Norway that he would study any Eskimos he met. The Eskimos were frightened at first. They had never seen white men. But they grew friendly. Soon there was a whole Eskimo village around the ship.

The Eskimos had a hard life in the Arctic cold. They wore furs, and under-wear of soft reindeer skin. Amundsen tried wearing it. He found it warmer than woolen underwear.

Amundsen traded with the Eskimos. He collected many of their tools for a museum in Norway. They had no iron so their tools were made of bone. In return he gave them wood for their sledges. He traded cooking pots for suits of fur.

The Eskimo women loved the pots. They would spend hours licking them. They cleaned everything by licking it! They wanted heavy needles too. For these they would trade fine skins.

The *Gjoa* stayed at Gjoahavn for two winters. It took that long to check their scientific observations. They found that the Northern Magnetic Pole did not stay in one place, but moved around.

While they were at Gjoahavn they explored nearby areas and mapped them. They studied the rocks and plants and animals. They kept records of the weather too. This was important, because polar weather affects the weather of the entire world.

In August, 1905, they had been at Gjoahavn for twenty months. Amundsen said, "We can sail now. The ice has melted enough." He took a deep breath. "Now we can hunt for the Northwest Passage."

6

The Northwest Passage at Last

Amundsen stood at the wheel of the *Gjoa*. It was his turn to steer. He watched the man at the bow "heaving the lead." A line weighted with lead was thrown over the side of the ship to find out how deep the water was.

They sailed carefully through the unknown waters. There was heavy fog and they could not see where they were. The man in the crow's nest peered into the fog.

"Ice ahead! Heavy ice on the port side!" he called out. Amundsen turned the little ship to the right.

"Too shallow here!" the man with the lead called out. Amundsen steered the ship to the left again.

The *Gjoa* went from side to side, twisting and turning. It was hard to find a way between the rocks and the ice. Sometimes it seemed she would surely go aground.

Each time they came to a group of islands, Amundson had to decide how to pass between them. The water was very shallow. If he made the wrong decision the whole expedition might be ruined.

Sometimes, when the lead was heaved, he hardly breathed. One time there was only an inch to spare between the *Gjoa's* bottom and the rocks!

For two weeks he worried, and could scarcely eat. Would they get through? Then, one morning, Lieutenant Hansen rushed into the cabin.

"Ship in sight, sir!" he cried.

Amundsen got up quickly. The ship ahead must have come from the Pacific. The *Gjoa* had sailed through the Northwest Passage!

Before Amundsen went on deck he stopped to look at a picture of his hero, Nansen, hanging on the wall. Did he imagine it, or did the picture nod to him? He seemed to hear a faint voice say, "Just what I thought, my boy!"

Soon the ship they had sighted came close. It was an American whaling ship. Amundsen was rowed over to her. The captain knew who Amundsen was. He said, "I am very pleased to be the first to welcome you on getting through the Northwest Passage." It was August 26, 1905.

The *Gjoa* sailed onward, dodging the ice and trying to get as far west as she could. But the weather was against them. Early in September they reached King Point, at the northwest corner of Canada. Beyond that they could not go. The ice was too thick. They would have to spend a third winter in the Arctic.

Amundsen wanted to get news of the *Gjoa's* achievement out to the world. He wanted the world to know about it.

The nearest telegraph office was hundreds of miles away. He met an American whaler captain whose ship had been crushed by the ice. This man wanted to get to San Francisco.

Amundsen went with him by dog sledge

to Eagle City in Alaska. There he sent out his telegrams. He waited two months for the mail from home. Then he went back to the *Gjoa*. Not until summer was the ship able to free herself from the ice.

The little *Gjoa* sailed on around Alaska. There were terrible storms. Finally they reached Nome and a hearty welcome from the Americans. Then they went down the coast to San Francisco.

7

A Change in Plans

The *Gjoa* was given to the city of San Francisco, and placed in a park. Amundsen returned to Norway.

What next? Why, the North Pole, of course! It was what he had always dreamed of. He wanted to be the first to reach it.

An American, Commander Robert E. Peary, was in the North, trying to reach it now. Many men had tried, and many had died in the effort.

Amundsen would do what the explorer Nansen had done. He would take a ship to the Arctic and let it drift with the ice and the sea currents. That way he could study them.

The ship would move so slowly he would have the chance to leave it and make a dash to the Pole. He would go by dog sled. Amundsen's eyes shone at the thought of the great adventure to come.

Nansen was pleased by his plans. He let Amundsen use his wonderful little ship, the *Fram*. "Fram" means "forward" in Norwegian. Amundsen was always going forward.

He chose his men and his supplies with care. This would be a long trip. It might take five years. There was no Panama Canal at that time. They would have to go south around the tip of South America. Then they would go north to Alaska and the Bering Strait. After that they would start to drift. The currents went from west to east.

In September, 1909, word came that Commander Peary had discovered the North Pole in April. This was a terrible blow to Amundsen.

"Will you go ahead with your plans now?" his brother asked him.

Amundsen shook his head. He had been downed, but not for long. "I have already changed my mind," he said. "I will try to reach the South Pole instead."

His brother frowned. "The Englishman, Captain Scott, is planning to do that," he reminded Amundsen.

"There is no reason why I cannot try too," Amundsen said. He added, "But I

would rather you didn't tell anyone of my change in plans."

The *Fram* sailed at last. Amundsen waited until the ship reached the island of Madeira, in the Atlantic. Then he called the crew on deck.

"I am going to try for the South Pole," he said. "If anyone doesn't want to go along, he can say so now."

A great shout went up. They all wanted to go along.

Before they left Madeira, Amundsen sent Captain Scott a cablegram. It said: "Am going south. Amundsen." Scott had already started south and was in Australia.

The trip was slow. When the men wanted amusement, they played with the dogs. There were 97 dogs on board. They were tied all over the deck.

Every time a dog was untied, it started a dog-fight. Then all the other dogs began to bark. Sometimes it was hard for Amundsen to hear himself think!

Lieutenant Nilsen was Amundsen's second-in-command. One day he said to Amundsen, "Do you think Scott will get to the Pole ahead of you?"

"Who knows?" Amundsen replied. "But I think we have a better chance. He's planning to use Siberian ponies and motor sledges for traveling. The motor sledges won't be practical on the ice and snow. And the ponies will suffer from the cold. How will he feed them?"

"I suppose he'll carry hay with him," Nilsen said.

Amundsen shook his head. "Dogs are better. They can eat seal meat and pemmican." Pemmican was dried meat and fat pressed into cakes. It was easy to carry.

"Of course dogs can fail, too," Amundsen went on. "But our dogs are used to polar work. They are quick, strong, and surefooted. They can go anywhere a man can go. And they are intelligent. I will pin my faith on the dogs."

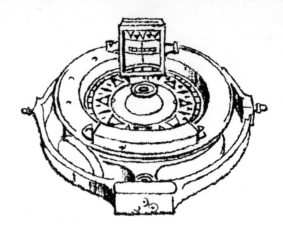

8

Preparing for the Trip

In January, 1911, they reached the Bay of Whales on the Antarctic continent. Ahead loomed a great wall of ice, the Ross Ice Barrier. They would make their base on top of the ice.

"We'll call our base Framheim," Amundsen said.

Soon the supplies and the dogs were unloaded. January was summer in the Antarctic. They would build their base

during the summer, spend the winter there, then start for the Pole in the spring. Wherever Scott was, he would have to do the same.

Early in February they had a great surprise. There, in the harbor, was another ship! It was the *Terra Nova*, Captain Scott's ship.

Scott was not aboard. He was at his base 400 miles away. Amundsen lunched with the officers of the *Terra Nova*. They talked of their plans, and Amundsen offered them some of his dogs. They did not take them, for they were counting on their ponies.

After a short visit, the *Terra Nova* left. Later the *Fram* sailed away. Her crew was to study the South Atlantic waters during the winter. She would return to Antarctica in October.

Amundsen and seven men were left at Framheim. A wooden hut had already been built, and tents set up. Now they dug more rooms under the snow and ice, and tunnels to connect them.

The dogs were happy, now that they were in their element of cold and snow. They romped and barked and fought. Each man had his own team of twelve dogs and had to train them.

Amundsen began to prepare for the trip to the Pole. He would set up supply depots along the first part of the route. Then it wouldn't be necessary to carry so much food on the final trip. The depots would be 70 miles apart.

The first one was reached in a few days. They marked the way with bamboo poles topped by black flags. These were easy to see in the snow. When they ran

out of bamboo poles they used frozen fish, stuck upright in the snow!

The second trip, to build the next two depots, was a hard one. The sledges were so heavily loaded the dogs could scarcely draw them. It was bitterly cold and very foggy.

Suddenly three of the leading dogs disappeared! They had fallen into a crevasse and were hanging by their harness. A crevasse is a deep crack in the ice or snow. The dogs were pulled up and the men went on.

On the way back to Framheim several of the dogs died. Amundsen felt badly, for they had given all of their strength to pulling the heavy sledges.

There was one more trip to the first depot, and then the long Antarctic winter was upon them.

They spent the six months studying the weather and improving their equipment. The sledges were made lighter, so they would be easier for the dogs to pull.

The men's boots were worked on so as to be completely comfortable. Few things would be more important than healthy feet when they made their dash for the Pole. It was all too easy to freeze toes and heels.

Eyes were important, too. All sorts of dark goggles were invented. The glare of the sun on the snow could cause blindness. Mittens, underwear, dogs, harnesses, packing cases—everything was studied and improved. When October came, they would be ready.

9

Danger in the Antarctic

On October 19, 1911, Amundsen and four men set out for the South Pole. There was Bjaaland, the best skier. There was Hanssen of the farseeing eyes, and Hassel who was the best dog-driver. There was Wisting, who had been with Amundsen on the *Gjoa*, and Amundsen himself. They took four sledges, and more than 50 dogs.

While they were gone, three men would explore along the coast.

The first day went well enough, but on the second they had a blizzard and it was hard to see. They had passed safely over several small crevasses when suddenly Bjaaland's sledge sank into a large one. He jumped off and held onto the rope. The dogs lay flat in the snow and braced themselves with their claws. The sledge was slowly dragging them down.

"Hurry! I can't hold it any longer!" Bjaaland cried.

The other men came running. They fastened a rope to the dogs' harness, then pulled them out. They could not pull up the sledge. It was too heavy.

They tied a rope around Wisting, and he was lowered over the side of the big crack. He tied other ropes to the cases

on the sledge. They were pulled up one by one. Then the sledge was light enough to get out.

Everywhere they looked there were crevasses. They seemed to be in a trap. They kept the dogs harnessed for safety.

"I'm going over to my sledge," Wisting called out.

Amundsen turned to watch him. Without any warning, Wisting's body disappeared. Only his head and shoulders were above the snow. He had fallen into a crevasse, but he had spread out his arms as he fell. It was quick thinking on his part that had saved him.

That afternoon the storm ended. Three of them tied themselves together with a rope. They set out on skis to find a way out of the trap. Everywhere they went were more crevasses.

"We'll have to turn back on our tracks," Amundsen said.

Soon they saw one of the guiding flags they had set up on their depot trips. The blizzard had thrown them off their course.

It took them almost a month of traveling to reach the mountains. There was more haze and fog, and plenty of snow. Other days the sunshine was so brilliant it hurt their eyes.

"We'll have to find a way through the mountains," Amundsen said. While the others made camp, he took two of his men to explore. The mountains were very high and the wind was bitter cold. In some places great masses of rock and ice barred the way. Sometimes avalanches of ice and snow roared down the mountain-side.

They found one pass which they thought

would do. Now to get the sledges up the mountains! The dogs did more than their share. In some places they could go only a few inches at a time. They crawled slowly upward on their bellies.

When they made camp, the men were tired. They were 11,000 feet above sea level. At that height there was much less oxygen in the air. That made them short of breath.

Before they were ready to go on, a blizzard was upon them. For four days they stayed in their tent. By the fifth day the men were restless. "Let's go," they said to Amundsen.

"It will be dangerous," he told them. "It's still storming."

"We don't care—let's go!"

He was just as eager to go as they were. Off they went. For days they traveled through the mountain ranges. Sometimes they climbed great ice sheets. Sometimes they hunted for a way through a maze of crevasses.

The weather was terrible. Much of the time they could not see where they were going! Noses and cheeks froze, but there was no time to stop. There was seldom time to make lunch. Dry biscuits and melted snow—that was lunch.

In early December they finally reached the high plain beyond the mountains. Only one man, Sir Ernest Shackleton, had been this far south, but on another route. After this point they would feel like real explorers.

10

The First to Reach the South Pole

On December 14, 1911, the men were as excited as boys at a ball game. Today they should reach the Pole! They kept a good watch for signs that other men had come this way. Had Scott and his expedition reached the Pole ahead of them? The country was bare of everything but snow and ice.

Suddenly, at three in the afternoon, the sledge-drivers shouted "Halt!" Their sledge-meters said they had reached their goal.

"This is the Pole?" one of the men asked. He added jokingly, "But there is nothing to mark the spot!"

"There will be," Amundsen said with a grin. He went to one of the sledges and lifted out the Norwegian flag.

"Come," Amundsen said, "we must put it up together." He wanted to show his thanks for all they had done.

Five frostbitten hands reached for the flagpole. As they pushed it into the snow, Amundsen said, *Thus we plant thee, beloved flag, at the South Pole, and give to the plain on which it lies the name of King Haakon VII's Plateau.*

It was a solemn moment. The men's

hearts filled with pride. They had done the impossible. They had reached the South Pole.

Amundsen sighed as they stepped back into line. All his life, from childhood on, he had wanted to travel to the North Pole. Yet here he was, at the other end of the earth!

That evening, in their tent, they celebrated. For 55 days they had eaten little else but pemmican, chocolate and biscuits. Tonight they had a little seal meat. It tasted delicious.

Huddled together in the warmth of the tent, they began to mark everything they had with them. The words "South Pole" were written on personal belongings for souvenirs. Not that the men would need souvenirs to help them remember this day!

Amundsen took out his pipe. That was to be marked, too, even though he had no tobacco for it.

"Here," Wisting held out his hand. "Take this, with my congratulations." Amundsen stared. This was a real reward —enough tobacco to smoke for the rest of the journey.

They stayed at the Pole for three days. The men explored in all directions, making observations. They made sure of the exact spot where the South Pole was located. They also made sure that Scott's men had not been there before them. Before they left, Amundsen set up a tent at the Pole. In it he left a note for Scott.

Scott found it on January 18, 1912. He had tried so hard to be the first, but Amundsen had been there before him. Scott and his men turned back. They

died of starvation and cold before they reached their base.

On their way back to Framheim, Amundsen and his men had better weather. They were so eager to get back that they went much faster than before.

On January 25, 1912, they reached their base. It was four in the morning and everyone in Framheim was asleep. Like children wanting to spring a surprise, Amundsen and his men stood outside. When they were together, they went in.

At first the men in the hut thought they were dreaming. There were the five explorers looking at them with grins on their faces.

"How about the Pole?" someone finally asked. "Have you been there?"

"Of course!" Amundsen tossed off the answer, trying to sound calm.

At that the cook leaped up. He put the coffeepot on. This was really a day for celebration. Amundsen and his men were home again. They had been gone 99 days and had traveled 1,860 miles to find the South Pole.

"For this," the cook said solemnly, "I think you deserve a cup of coffee!"

11

Bad Luck

Amundsen often said, "Exploration from the air is the coming thing."

He was so sure of it that he bought a plane and learned to fly it. He planned to take it with him on his new ship, the *Maud*. He had designed the ship himself. He was going to try to drift across the Polar Sea to the North Pole.

"You are a stubborn Norseman," his friends told him.

"Of course I am. You have to be stubborn to explore in the Polar regions," Amundsen said.

World War I started and spoiled his plans. He gave his plane to the Norwegian government. It was not until 1918 that he could start his voyage with the *Maud*. He would go north of Norway, then along the north coast of Europe and Asia. There he would join the Arctic current and drift to the Pole

Bad luck struck almost at once. The *Maud* was caught in the ice north of Asia and had to stay there for a whole year.

One cold morning, when Amundsen was on the runway between the ship and the ice, one of the dogs ran toward him. Amundsen tripped over the dog. The fall broke his right shoulder. That was bad enough, but worse was to come.

A few weeks later he went for a walk near the ship. Suddenly he saw Jakob, the *Maud's* watchdog, running for his life. Behind him came a mother polar bear.

The bear saw Amundsen. There was nothing to do but run for the ship. Amundsen lost the race! The bear struck him on the back, and Amundsen fell on his broken shoulder. Now, he thought, I shall be killed!

The dog had reached the ship. When he saw the bear standing over Amundsen, he went for the bear's cub. The bear turned from Amundsen and went for Jakob. With a prayer of thanksgiving, Amundsen got up and ran aboard the *Maud*. It was a very narrow escape.

He had another narrow escape a short time afterward. He was nearly overcome by the fumes from a kerosene lamp. He had been working in a small room where there was no fresh air.

Suddenly he felt his heart beating too hard and too fast. He managed to get outside. But he was weak for a long time.

In September, 1919, the ship was freed from the ice. But they were in open water less than two weeks. Then the ship was held fast in the ice again. After ten long months she was freed. The expedition went to Nome, Alaska, for supplies and repairs.

At Nome four men decided to leave the expedition. Two had quit earlier. That left only four men to work the ship. Amundsen asked five Eskimos to help.

There seemed no end to their bad luck. The *Maud's* propeller broke. Amundsen went back to Norway to raise money for more supplies.

When he returned to Alaska he brought an airplane and a pilot with him. Amundsen planned to fly over the polar sea and study the air currents. His findings would help scientists to understand weather changes.

They tried out the plane in Alaska. The plane's skis broke when they landed. Amundsen decided that a plane would need pontoons in the Arctic, so it could land in water. That meant getting another plane. Pontoons would not fit on this one.

Amundsen was no business man, and he knew it. He hired a business manager to help him with his plans. Unfortunately the man he chose ran up a lot of bills. There was no money to pay them. Amundsen went bankrupt.

This was the low point of his life. He came to the United States and tried to

make money by writing and giving talks. He owed so much money he was in despair.

Then the telephone rang, and a voice said, "I am Lincoln Ellsworth. I am an amateur interested in exploration. I might be able to supply some money for another expedition."

Amundsen's spirits rose. Lincoln Ellsworth was a rich man. For the first time in months Amundsen saw hope ahead.

12

Amundsen Takes
to the Air

Amundsen and Ellsworth planned to fly across the polar sea. Ellsworth bought two flying boats and named them *N-24* and *N-25*. Amundsen found the pilots and mechanics for them. The six men met at Spitzbergen, north of Norway.

First, they decided to make a shorter flight. They wanted to see if there were any places where flying boats could land.

They left Spitzbergen on May 21, 1925, and flew north over the ice. There was enough gasoline in their tanks to go 600 miles and back. They flew almost the entire 600 miles before they saw any open water.

They circled lower to look at it. Suddenly the *N-24* developed engine trouble. It managed to land in the little stretch of water. The *N-25* landed not far away.

Almost at once the little strip of water froze solid. That was bad.

Amundsen took stock. They had food for only three weeks. The *N-24's* engine would not work. That meant that all six men would have to be carried in the *N-25*. It would be overloaded. And how would they get off the ice?

It was in times like these that Amundsen's great qualities appeared. He knew the dangers of the Arctic, but he did not despair. Instead he set to work to figure out a way to save the expedition.

They would have to have a runway. "But the ice is too rough," said the pilot. "Look at those big hummocks heaped together, no matter where you turn."

"We'll have to flatten them out," Amundsen said cheerfully. "And we'll have to do it in a hurry."

He knew, better than any of the others, that this was a race with death. They had only eight ounces of food a day. The work was terribly hard. In 24 days they moved more than 500 tons of ice to make their runway.

At its end was a sharp drop to a pool of water. Beyond that was a hummock twenty feet high. They had neither the time nor the strength to break that down.

When the pilot took off, the rough runway made the plane sway from side to side. If it tipped too far, a wing might be crushed. Amundsen held his breath as the end of the runway neared.

The plane cleared the pool. Would it get over the big hummock? Everyone in the plane was motionless. Only the pilot moved. He pulled hard on the stick.

They were over! "I don't think there was an inch to spare," Amundsen said.

The trip back was one of suspense. Did they have enough fuel? Would they have to land on the ice?

Suddenly a shout went up from the six men. The mountains of Spitzbergen were in sight! At the very last one of the controls failed. Once more Amundsen held his breath. But they landed safely in the water. They were home again!

13

Last Adventures

Amundsen was still sure that flying was the best way to explore polar regions. But he felt a dirigible would be better than a plane.

A dirigible is a long, cigar-shaped balloon with cabins hanging underneath. It has motors and can be steered. In those days dirigibles were safer than airplanes. They could fly farther too.

Ellsworth bought a dirigible from the Italian government. They named it the *Norge*, for Norway. They planned to leave from Spitzbergen again, and fly over the North Pole to Alaska.

Since they did not know how to fly a dirigible, they hired Colonel Nobile to do it for them. Colonel Nobile was the Italian officer who had designed the *Norge*. He was a vain, jealous man and very excitable.

"I wish we had anyone else for the job," Amundsen said to Ellsworth.

Ellsworth did not like Nobile, either. "But we have to have him," he said with a sigh.

A few days before the *Norge* was ready to leave, the American flyer Commander Richard Byrd arrived at Spitzbergen with his plane. Byrd and his

mechanic, Floyd Bennett, flew to the North
Pole and back again. They were the first
to reach it by air. Amundsen and his
friends greeted them warmly. Amundsen
was not jealous. His goal was different.
He planned to map the polar seas.

On May 11, 1926, everything was
ready, and the *Norge* rose into the air.
The crew was part Norwegian and part
Italian. Ellsworth took observations to
study the electricity in the air. Amundsen
kept a constant watch for any signs of
land. At that time no one knew if there
was an Arctic continent or not.

Nobody had much sleep during the 72
hours of flight. There was too much to
do, too much to see. When they were
over the North Pole, they dropped the
flags of their countries. Amundsen must
have sighed a little, remembering his

former ambition. Now, at last, he was at the North Pole, only he was far above it!

Later Ellsworth said, "Do you recognize anything below?"

Amundsen smiled. "Those are islands I visited on the *Gjoa*. How different they look from the air!"

When they reached Alaska, Amundsen was satisfied with the results of the trip. They had been the first to cross the Arctic. Again he had done something which had never been done before.

All through his life he had worked hard and planned carefully. No matter what the difficulties, he had persevered. He felt that this trip was the climax of his career as an explorer.

"Now I shall retire," he told his friends. "I have books to write and talks to give. If I can be of any help to young explorers—well, they know where to find me."

Two years later Nobile had a new airship, the *Italia*. He said that *he* was going to be an explorer. He flew over the North Pole again. But this time his dirigible was headed for disaster. The *Italia* plunged down onto the ice. The ten men aboard were helpless.

Amundsen disliked Nobile. But at once he made plans to go to the rescue.

France offered him a fine plane with a pilot and a crew of three. "It is just what I need," Amundsen told his friends.

"But *you* are not going, are you?" one of them asked.

"Not going?" Amundsen echoed in real surprise. "I must go. I know the North. I may be of some help."

His plane flew off. Nobile was rescued, but not by Amundsen. Roald Amundsen and his brave crew disappeared into the North. They were never found.

It was the way Amundsen would have wanted to die. It was a fitting death for one of Norway's greatest heroes.

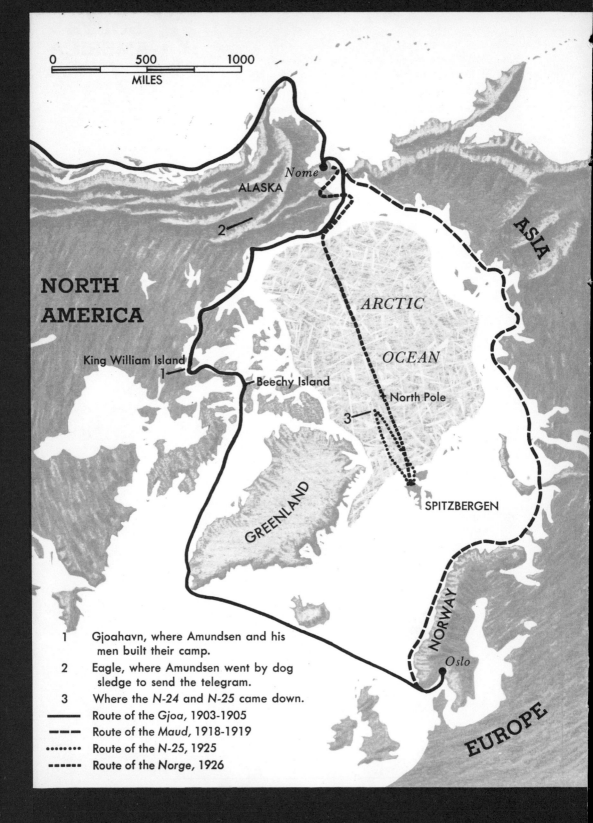

0 500 1000
MILES

Nome

ALASKA

2

NORTH
AMERICA

ARCTIC

OCEAN

King William Island

1

Beechy Island

North Pole

3

GREENLAND

SPITZBERGEN

ASIA

NORWAY

Oslo

EUROPE

1   Gjoahavn, where Amundsen and his
      men built their camp.
2   Eagle, where Amundsen went by dog
      sledge to send the telegram.
3   Where the *N-24* and *N-25* came down.
————   Route of the *Gjoa*, 1903-1905
– – –   Route of the *Maud*, 1918-1919
••••••••   Route of the *N-25*, 1925
– – – –   Route of the *Norge*, 1926